Confessions of a Reiki Exorcist

Confessions of a Reiki Exorcist

Damon Corrie

Published by Damon Corrie, 2021.

CONFESSIONS OF A REIKI EXORCIST

First edition. September 17, 2021.

Copyright © 2021 Damon Corrie.

ISBN: 979-8201011789

Written by Damon Corrie.

Table of Contents

This book is dedicated to my Reiki Master - Mrs. Janice Chin Worme and her son - Quantum touch Master Joseph Chin, who has been one of my best friends and teachers for most of my life.

CHAPTER 1

INTRODUCTION

Most Reiki light workers do NOT get involved in exorcisms, many do not even want to confront evil and break spells, it is just too dangerous, either you - or your loved ones, or at the very least - your pets, often pay the price for your working against the powers and principalities of spiritual darkness in positions of power all over this world. But this was my calling from birth, not everyone in my family is happy, because they have suffered the backlash in various ways, but my moral dilemma is - should I use my spiritual gift and continue to help those afflicted - who are so overjoyed when they obtain relief after years of suffering ? Or do I ignore my gift and let others continue to suffer because I am afraid that my loved ones may be harmed? What would you do - if you were me?

———◉———

Additionally, as a someone who habitually cures himself only using natural remedies and natural energy since I turned 40, I want the reader to know that I am neither a pro-vaccine nor anti-vaccine fanatic, and I don't go around thinking that I have a monopoly on the 'truth', so I do not insult the intelligence of anyone who wants to get vaccinated - nor do I insult the intelligence of anyone who refuses to get vaccinated.

I believe in two things according to how I was raised and trained as a lightworker, #1 - RESPECT for the opinions and convictions of others - because EVERYONE formulates their own opinions and perspectives on life, based upon the times, circumstances, and experiences that have characterized their own existence, and the information they have gathered for themselves, so in each person's mind - they have reached an 'informed' opinion, and technically - indeed they have (according to their own observed reality)...therefore who am I (or you) to tell ANYONE else that they are 'absolutely wrong' and you (or I) are 'absolutely right'?

———◉———

How can you expect anyone to forget all they have learned in their lives up to this point, just because YOU are now telling them that their perspective is wrong - and yours is 'right'? One cannot learn by forgetting.

This kind of egotistical stance is not a demonstration of the superiority of your academic intelligence or wisdom as you may have assumed, but instead is only a demonstration of your arrogance, and LACK of wisdom...for you are showing utter disregard and contempt for other human beings and their individual thought processes, and the universally recognised dignity and rights of every human being, your fellow man, your spiritual sisters and brothers.

Freely share the information that you have accumulated with others if you wish, but do so with dignity and respect for the self-worth of everyone else foremost in your mind, not the ego-driven desire to 'win the argument', otherwise, you will never LISTEN in order to LEARN anything, you will only listen to respond, and this is the opposite of wisdom and any genuine personal possession of 'high intellect' on your part.

I have seen people I know on social media insulting the intelligence of those who do not share their position on vaccinations, I even know some people who have become so mentally tyrannical (in their own fear-based minds), that they support the imprisonment of those who refuse to be vaccinated.

$$\Longrightarrow \textbf{\textcolor{black}{\bullet}} \Longleftarrow$$

So when I give them emotionless LEGAL arguments (based on my 16 years of Human Rights work in the Organization of American States/OAS, and 13 years of Human Rights work in the United Nations Permanent Forum on Indigenous Issues/UNPFII) on why every human being has enshrined legal rights to request OR refuse vaccinations (based on their own free prior and informed consent principle), they resort to emotion-driven responses that hold no weight in any court of law anywhere, with such low brow retorts as 'rights, what rights? where were my human rights when this or that bad thing happened to me in my life' (which is totally beside the point and judicially irrelevant), or they make false comparisons such as 'people don't like wearing seat belts but once it was made national law they had to accept it and it has been for our own good'...yes seatbelts have proven to be life-savers, but when you stop driving your car - you can take off your seat belt, but when you put a vaccine into your body - you cannot take it back out - HUGE DIFFERENCE.

FYI - As a side note, forced vaccinations became illegal under International law after the Nuremberg trials (November 20th, 1945 - October 1st, 1946) of the surviving captured Nazi leaders after World War 2, because the Nazis were infamous for conducting forced vaccinations on captive populations they considered to be 'sub-human' such as the Jews, Gypsies, etc, so the victorious allies from western democracies - decreed that never again would any government or individual be allowed to force vaccinations on any human being anywhere for any reason, so the legal facts I mention are not some 'new age woke crap', its ACTUALLY enshrined in International Human Rights Laws and Conventions, not based on any emotion-driven personal opinions - or profit-driven Pharmaceutical Industry agendas.

CHAPTER 2

I flew from Barbados island in the Caribbean (my birthplace) on Friday 23rd July 2021 to Guyana, South America (birthplace of my grandmother and maternal ancestors, my wife, and 4 of our 5 children), I traveled overland from the capital city of Georgetown for 400 miles (which took 16 hours on mud trails we frequently got stuck in) to donate mini portable solar panel light kits to every home that was without light - in the Indigenous Makushi Tribal Nation village of Toka, in region 9, near the Brazil border in South Western Guyana.

———— ◉ ————

I did this on behalf of the 3 Indigenous NGOs that I co-founded and co-lead - like the Caribbean Amerindian Development Organization/ CADO, and the Indigenous Democracy Development Organization/ IDDO, and also the United Confederation of Taino People - of which I am a Board member.

———— ◉ ————

I only stayed 3 days to accomplish this, with the assistance of my youngest brother-in-law Cleveland Simon from Pakuri village, in one of my own Lokono-Arawak Tribal Nations territories in region 4, northern Guyana.

Toka Village is nestled at the foothills of the southern range of the Pakaraima mountains in Guyana, one could describe it as being the second gateway to the Pakaraima mountains - if you are heading north from the Rupununi Region, or the second gateway to the North Rupununi Savannahs - if you are heading south from the Pakaraima mountains. With another bigger Makushi Tribal Nation village called Karasabai - being the first and better known gateway.

I prefer Toka personally, for historic reasons, as the dominant family clan here - were integral and fiercely loyal allies of my own great-great-great grandfather who was the Hereditary Chief of our Eagle Clan of the Lokono-Arawak people, back in 1850, when we were still engaged in intertribal wars, the ancestors of this dominant Toka family Clan (Davis & Isaac - are their Christianised surnames now) - fought bravely alongside my own ancestors, because my ancestor had taken a daughter of their Chief as his wife - and thereby secured a military alliance with those Makushis, who were at that time not living where Toka is now, but were living in a mountain top village - where no enemy could approach them without being seen beforehand.

Toka is also blessed with abundant mega fauna wildlife today, and I take visitors there on combined Adventure,Culture, and nature based - 7-14 day adventures often.

Our bus got stuck in the mud trail highway 6 times in 400 miles

Handing over the Solar light kit donations to Chief Micah Davis of Toka Village, Makushi Territory. The author at right, and IDDO Territorial Commander ex-Chief Stoby Davis at left. The IDDO has an indigenous paramilitary wing that operates in multiple countries - which I created and lead, called the IDDO Foreign Legion, in accordance with International Law - we engage in non-lethal activities such as training indigenous community Police groups and provide uniforms to them, and we offer basic community defence tactical training for indigenous communities in conflict zones, etc.

For example, in Panama, Central America, the IDDO Foreign Legion has helped teach one Embera Tribal Community the art of basic marksmanship, and community based self-defence skills and tactics, and donated equipment to this end to the community as well. You can look for the Indigenous Democracy Defence Organization on Facebook.

In northern Iraq, the IDDO Foreign Legion has assisted the long oppressed Yazidi indigenous people in various ways as well, since 2017.

We departed Toka and traveled by road again on Wednesday, July 28th to the regional capital city of Lethem Town on the Guyana side of the Brazil river border, to the home in St. Ignatius Indigenous Village of my older Lokono-Arawak friend James La Rose & his Makushi & Wapishana mixed wife Ann-Marie Paulinho-La-Rose, we stayed there only one night before flying back from Lethem to Georgetown on Thursday, July 29th. However, on Friday, July 30th Ann-Marie told me that she and her husband and her 2 youngest daughters - Saana & Mayau (whom they asked me to name as babies), had just tested positive for the 'crown' virus that morning (Friday), so I went for a test at Eureka Labs in Georgetown that same day to see if I was infected as well.

Ann-Marie Paulinho La Rose

Author at far left, in middle is James La Rose, at far right is Cleveland
Simon

Saana La Rose with the author on the morning of Thursday 29th July 2021

Mayau La Rose with the author on the morning of Thursday 29th July 2021

CHAPTER 3

On Saturday 31st July I collected my results and I was negative. Cleveland did not bother to test himself as he is vaccinated with the Russian Sputnik vaccine. I however remain unvaccinated, as I have the inner conviction that I am healthy enough to withstand and survive any strain of crown virus that fate allows to befall me.

———— ◉ ————

The negative results coupled with ego made me feel bold, that I could literally be having meals and taking close embracing photos with virus victims and still not get infected, but my friend Ronald Taggoa in the Philippines reminded me that the crown virus can hide in your system for up to 14 days before symptoms emerged...and he was right.

———— ◉ ————

On Sunday 1st August 2021 I flew from Guyana to Barbados in the morning, then along with my fellow Lokono-Arawak wife of 28 years - Shirling (46), and our youngest daughter Laliwa (14), we all flew from Barbados to Antigua the same evening.

———— ◉ ————

However, it was on Thursday 5th August - while walking back from a beach in Antigua, with my wife and daughter, that I suddenly felt faint, as if I was going to blackout and fall into the road, so I quickly sat on a roadside wall and told my wife "Babe, I don't feel right, something is wrong", at first we thought it was sunstroke - as I was not wearing a hat, and it was a very hot sunny day, but I never wear hats - and it's always hot and sunny in the Caribbean, and even hotter and sunnier in Guyana closer to the equator -where I routinely walk 30 miles a day without a hat, in the blazing sun, across savannas devoid of water or shade....so it could not be that.

———— ◉ ————

I then told my wife "maybe my Malaria is acting up again - as it feels similar to my last Malaria outbreak", but then I second-guessed that also because even though doctors told me that the Malaria parasites would incubate in my body forever - and COULD break out in my body again at any time (and that's why I cannot donate my blood to anyone), but the fact that I never had such a Malaria outbreak before since my last infection over 20 years ago - made me doubt it could be Malaria either.

———————◉———————

I began to wonder if I had caught the crown virus, but then on Friday morning 6th August, we all collected our Antigua Lab test results which we did on Wednesday 4th August, and we were all negative, so my wife and daughter thought it can't be the virus either.

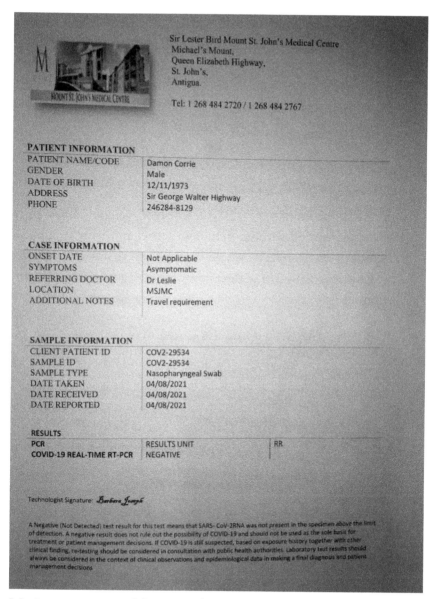

Sir Lester Bird Mount St. John's Medical Centre
Michael's Mount,
Queen Elizabeth Highway,
St. John's,
Antigua.

Tel: 1 268 484 2720 / 1 268 484 2767

PATIENT INFORMATION

PATIENT NAME/CODE	Damon Corrie
GENDER	Male
DATE OF BIRTH	12/11/1973
ADDRESS	Sir George Walter Highway
PHONE	246284-8129

CASE INFORMATION

ONSET DATE	Not Applicable
SYMPTOMS	Asymptomatic
REFERRING DOCTOR	Dr Leslie
LOCATION	MSJMC
ADDITIONAL NOTES	Travel requirement

SAMPLE INFORMATION

CLIENT PATIENT ID	COV2-29534
SAMPLE ID	COV2-29534
SAMPLE TYPE	Nasopharyngeal Swab
DATE TAKEN	04/08/2021
DATE RECEIVED	04/08/2021
DATE REPORTED	04/08/2021

RESULTS

PCR	RESULTS UNIT	RR
COVID-19 REAL-TIME RT-PCR	NEGATIVE	

Technologist Signature: *Barbara Joseph*

A Negative (Not Detected) test result for this test means that SARS- CoV-2RNA was not present in the specimen above the limit of detection. A negative result does not rule out the possibility of COVID-19 and should not be used as the sole basis for treatment or patient management decisions. If COVID-19 is still suspected, based on exposure history together with other clinical finding, re-testing should be considered in consultation with public health authorities. Laboratory test results should always be considered in the context of clinical observations and epidemiological data in making a final diagnosis and patient management decisions

My Antigua negative lab test result

There were no more symptoms so we all figured it was a one-off stomach bug or some other darn thing, so we continued on our planned 3 week holiday - and flew to Sint Maarten on the night of Friday 6th

August 2021 for what we expected to be the latter 2 weeks, all happy and
excited to visit that friendly destination (for the second time this year -
as my wife and I were there for 5 weeks around Easter time), where all
one needs is a negative test less than 72 hours old (which we had from
Antigua) and you walk straight out of the airport and begin your Sint
Maarten holiday.

———————⊙———————

Unlike most other Caribbean destinations that impose an immediate
7-14 days quarantine AT YOUR EXPENSE - upon arrival, and who
in their right mind without money to waste, and with a limited 7-21
days annual vacation leave, would choose to go to any other Caribbean
island and lose 1/3 - 2/3 of their entire annual vacation time in damned
quarantine?

———————⊙———————

Certainly not me, that's why I prefer to go to islands like Sint Maarten
that have great beaches, jungle-covered mountains, cheap tasty food,
lots to do and see with friendly locals, and a cheaper bigger variety
of shopping than any other Caribbean island (because it's a duty-free
country) - only Panama can compare favorably in these latter regards.

———————⊙———————

Then, on Sunday, August 8th - mild symptoms began to show, slight
pain behind the eyes - but very mild - so I chalked it up to mere fatigue,
and a dry cough - but again a literal 'one cough' and stop affair, just
2-3 times a day, so I thought it was just dust in the 2 story house we
were renting in Sint Maarten - even though visually it looks spic and
span - because you cannot truly dust-proof any house in the Caribbean
unless you keep all windows and doors closed 24/7 and run the expensive
Air-Conditioning around the clock at least 10 months of the year
(February to November).

———— ◉ ————

Then the third symptom of nightly fevers began as well, but again, so mild that I ignored them, no waking up in sweats or trembling with cold feelings - nothing exceptional like that, as these are the things that would ring alarm bells in anyone's mind, especially someone like me who does not even get colds, as I rarely if ever gets infected...I only get infested lol.

FYI As a side note, my former family doctor - Malcolm Grant (now a very pro-vaccine gentleman in the current debate) literally once told me "Damon, I have learned more about tropical parasites and bacteria from you than from all my years in University studying medicine".

———— ◉ ————

In his time with us in my ages from 20-30 - I had both types of the Malaria parasite, I had Amoebic dysentery, I had an Amazonian flesh-eating bacteria that he had to insert his entire index finger a whole 2 inches into the hole in my upper leg the bacteria had eaten out of me, to put a pus absorbing plug into my muscle tissue, and I remember this because Dr. Grant told me he was surprised I did not show any sign of being in severe pain as he did so because he said the pain equivalent of what he was doing - would be taking a .22 bullet to my leg at point-blank range.

———— ◉ ————

I suspect, like my 3 older children - who inherited it from me, I have a high threshold for physical pain, probably from their mum also - because she gave birth 5 times naturally without an epidural, and not once did she ever cry out in pain during childbirth.

———— ◉ ————

It's not the traditional way of our people to cry out in pain, only the person who bears pain with stoicism is respected, and there are intergenerational trauma reasons for this - for when we were constantly being attacked by enemies (which only ended just over a century ago), if you were wounded (for example) and hiding and you made noise - your enemies would find you, and if you were wounded and hiding with others who were trying to save you and themselves - your inability to tolerate your pain in silence would become a death sentence for you and everyone hiding nearby as well.

―――◉―――

So in the tribe you always put WE before ME, you as an individual tribal member are never worth more than the tribal collective as a macro blood family whole.

―――◉―――

Getting back to my recent virus tribulation, the first week was marked by slowly increasing mild symptoms, and I continued to eat cooked food - albeit in half or quarter portions than normal, but the second week - THAT really stuck the pin in the party hog let me tell you!

―――◉―――

From Saturday 14th August, in what was supposed to be our second and last week of vacation in Sint Maarten, the one severe crown virus symptom I had - manifested, severe breathing difficulties.

―――◉―――

I would get up from laying flat sleeping on our bed in the morning and have to spend 10 minutes regularising my breath - from fast shallow 'I can barely breathe' inhalations, to normal breathing, then a short walk to the toilet bowl, for my usual morning bowel movements, which required the same 10 minutes to regularise my breathing every time I stood up.

―――◉―――

Then I would brush my teeth, then weakly walk about 20 feet to the living room to sit on the sofa, and when I sat down - same 10 minutes to catch my breath, and so it went, a week of no energy, sleeping most of the day away, pain to breathe and difficulty breathing, no appetite due to a coated tongue, etc.

But on my last night of this crap, I reached my one and only low point, I had attempted to get up off the sofa to head to bed, and I could hardly breathe or even speak (and folks having an asthma attack would know the feeling - though I never had any breathing conditions hitherto in my entire 47 years of life), I had to signal with hand gestures - for my wife and daughter to do Reiki on me (as I was too feeble to do Reiki on myself properly) and run natural energy through my lungs to help me breathe, they did and I eventually felt relief, but not before I heard my wife and young daughter sobbing - as at this stage they realized daddy could die from this, combined viral and supernatural attack, and hearing them surrender to despair - just broke me emotionally, so all I could do was cover my eyes with my right hand, and with trembling lips - I too wept with them.

The author and his family in 2017- his wife, two sons, and two daughters (including then 11-year-old Laliwa - one of the youngest Reiki degree holders in the world)- ALL of whom are Usui Reiki Natural Energy degree holders, but only father Damon is a level 3 practitioner, daughter Sabantho is level 2, and everyone else is level 1. It is, in fact, the only family known outside of Japan whose every member is a Usui Reiki degree holder.

CHAPTER 4

This was the culmination of a week of distress, however, there were several supernatural occurrences in this second week when my decline was at its most severe, by this time I was no longer eating cooked food - as I had lost my appetite, and the coated tongue did not help either, but I still was able to eat fruit every day, one orange, plums, nectarines, mangos, peaches, grapes, pears, watermelon, avocado, bananas, etc. And I was drinking only water - that I blessed myself, as i'll teach you to do later in this book.

———⊚———

From a health note point, I realized and observed in mental notes, that when you eat ONLY fruit, your flatulence reduces - and it literally becomes odorless, I would be sitting next to my wife and pass gas, and she would not notice - because it was odorless, and she of all people knows - normally when I eat cooked food, I can clear a room real fast when I let one rip.

———⊚———

Obviously, our body can process natural fruit perfectly, but not cooked food, hence why our remotest ancestors were predominantly foragers gathering seasonal fruit and edible plants (and why many species of primate - including the great Apes who share 97% of our DNA - STILL primarily eat a raw fruit and plant-based diet).

———⊚———

It reminded me of the words of an old Shaman in Amazonia I trained under, who looked young and fit despite his advanced years, in his 80's he was still climbing trees to pick fruit, and he told me 'Fruit is the only food that is completely natural and alive (at a molecular level) even after you pick it (as long as you leave it unfrozen or unheated), and your body absorbs it completely, it is life-giving you life, but cooked food is mostly destroyed (at a molecular level) so only a part of it can be used by the body, the rest is turned into waste"...obviously he was telling me the truth, as for the men's sexual health perspective:

———◉———

The interest was still there - so early in the second week my wife and I tried to make love, as even after 28 years of marriage - it's still a nightly joint interest of ours (barring menstruation or serious illness), she was able to 'achieve her objective', but I was not, as I had to stop after satisfying her because I could hardly breathe.

———◉———

So as not to have to return to this subject later on in the text, I'll jump forward to the 1st day of the 3rd week, when I KNEW that I was on the road to recovery.

How did I know this? Well among other reasons that I will discuss shortly that are not of an adult nature, I awoke on Monday morning 30th August 2021 with my usual morning erection once again, a literal tear of joy rolled down my cheek as I exclaimed 'YES! We are back in business again!"

I had not had a morning erection since the week before, and I began to think I would have to buy and start to wear a black tie, as I do not own nor wear any ties - but I recalled old Great Uncle Keith once telling me in jest - that the day I see him wearing a black-tie - I'll know that his penis is dead.

———◉———

As for the supernatural issues, here are some of the most noteworthy incidents in that second week of gloom:

———◉———

I was asleep and I woke up to see a huge entity strangling me, its arm was bigger than my upper leg, for some reason the word 'Nephilim' came into my thoughts, I began praying in my mind - but it was having no effect, and I felt the energy draining from me, then I remembered that words have power, as thought becomes spoken word - which becomes manifested into reality, so with my last ebbing strength I was just able to speak my prayer in a low tone between breaths, it then the entity disappeared.

———————⬤———————

Another point I would like to share with the reader, which might be a bit difficult to understand, is that human beings - unlike the rest of creation, have a 'holy trinity' of a mortal physical body, an energetic carbon copy of our body - called our spirit, and an immortal conscious energy called our soul. All other living things have the first two - but only we have the 3rd component of the soul. Holy wisdom teachers have tried to explain this and been misunderstood for millennia.

For example, a man died in an accident, his body is dead, but his spirit which looks exactly like his physical body - was seen at the accident spot, and was seen in his house and various other places his body frequented when it was alive, this is because your spirit (being an energetic carbon copy of your body) ALSO has the same information/knowledge that the body had up to the point of physical death, so your soul can and will linger on the Earth and appear and even speak to its still living loved ones. But the SOUL of that man is long gone, what belongs to God cannot be trapped on the Earthplane by anyone, it is untouchable, but your spirit can be, that's why people see the person's spirit 'haunting' a place, no, it is just lingering in the places it knew in life.

These discarded energetic carbon copies of the once living body CAN be summoned or trapped by occultists, they can also be imitated by evil entities, so be aware of that.

It is also a mistake to pray in your mind only, always remember to speak your prayers as words have power, that is also why the servants of the darkness likewise do not merely think evil thoughts directed against you, they speak their evil words - this is how they cast spells, so the power of words is a double-edged sword, it cuts both ways, because always in this perception of reality - there exists a balance, as much good is always occurring on the Earth as evil is occurring, and as yet - good is not triumphing everywhere at all times - and neither is evil.

———— ◉ ————

We all hope for the day when only good manifests, well, at least the servants of the light do; because we have not forgotten that we come from the love and light - and it is there we desire to return one day after learning all that it is to be human, for what humanity experiences - cannot be experienced in the spirit world in the presence of the Creator, no pain, no hunger, no thirst, no discontent, no envy, no physical intimacy, no negative thoughts or emotions whatsoever, only peace and love and a divine bliss one cannot describe adequately in human terms in any way that can be fully comprehended here.

———— ◉ ————

This is why it is utter folly to say such things as "I will hate that person till I die" or "I will hate that person forever, I will never forgive them".

———— ◉ ————

Do you not realize that you cannot re-enter a place of divine perfection with any karmic trace of human imperfection in you? By holding on to hate - no matter what evils were inflicted upon you or loved ones - you only harm yourself, not the person who committed the evil act/s. They will atone for their own deeds, I assure you.

———— ◉ ————

Rest assured, everyone WILL answer for their ill deeds, just as surely as everyone will be rewarded for their good deeds in each human lifetime, it is not your place or mine to become judge, jury, and executioner of any other soul, only that which created it has that divine right.

———— ◎ ————

This is a very hard lesson for humans to learn, that is why Jesus said "many will hear my words - but few can bear to follow them". Contrary to popular belief, if you are a person who is comfortable with the baggage of sin, it will seem like the hardest task in the world to live a less sinful life, but this is precisely what must be done if you ever hope to become worthy again of reentering the presence of our divine creator.

———— ◎ ————

I am not saying that you have to be a sinless saint to receive blessings and abilities, look at the ordinary people Jesus and other righteous prophets all over the world selected to be their disciples, all of them had negative karmic baggage, or in other words - they were all people who had committed many sins in their lives, just like you and I.

———— ◎ ————

I was born under the Zodiac sign of Scorpio, and even though I don't have any interest in Astrology, I did notice that all the traits they ascribe to Scorpio people - were spot on in my case, and it took a lot of personal work to begin to shed all my negative Scorpio traits (and i'm not done shedding all of them yet!) and try to live in a way that serves the highest good of myself and others. In a nutshell, one has to take responsibility for everything in YOUR world, and by that I mean - recognise and understand that you are not separate from the rest of humanity and the natural world, you are connected to it all, when you put out positive vibrations - they not only come back to you, but they spread out into the universe first like the butterfly effect. Same goes for negative vibrations.

I would also like every reader to commit to memory - that It is a mistake to pray in your mind only, always remember to speak your prayers as words have power, have a one on one direct personal conversation with God, no intermediaries are needed, and you do not have to go to any special location to have this prayerful conversation with God, it can occur at any time in any place..just be cognizant that you must be sincere and respectful, just as you would if you were talking to someone you greatly loved, admired, and respected, you are not Gods equal, you are an inferior being speaking to a superior being, never forget that.

In the nights, during my viral attack, smirking dark entities would come and give me deadly false advice, like telling me to cut myself and the bloodletting would cure me, and I would tell them to get away from me with their stupid advice - because they only wanted to hasten my demise, and I could tell they were of the darkness and not of the light. On other previous occasions, young, stunningly gorgeous and very sexually attractive female Demons have appeared to me, they always try to use my high libido Scorpio primal nature - to tempt me, but when I look carefully, there is always something 'wrong' about their body, if it isn't their teeth, they have the withered hands of an old woman (or claws instead of nails), or beastly feet - or claws instead of toenails, always some giveaway that reveals their true demonic nature if you examine them carefully.

Im not gay so ofcourse I give them a look over, but I never let them trick me into sex.

One great misconception that the average religious devotee believes, is that 'only people who do evil see evil things'...have they not read of the temptation of Christ in the desert for 40 days? In reality, there are two ways that guarantee that you will see evil/lower vibrational entities, #1 - if you are serving evil - you will naturally be surrounded by evil and see evil entities continuously because you are helping them.

———◈———

However, if #2 - you are working against evil, you also will see evil entities appear to you intermittently, because you are harming them - therefore you become a dangerous enemy to them, so they appear to you in order to defeat you by fear, or if that fails - they up the ante - and try to inflict or cause physical harm to you or your loved ones - or even your pets.

———◈———

In my most unforgettable incident with demonic entities BEFORE I learned Shamanic and Reiki Natural Energy skills, my eldest son Hatuey (then a teenager) was involved, 3 female demons manifested after we fell asleep listening to techno music, I recall it was a monotonous beat only - no lyrics, and the track (we were sure we never heard before) just kept repeating, but we were too lazy to get up and walk across the room to turn it off.

The 3 attractive demons called me outside pretending to be lost tourists needing help, being a typical male I did not think 3 short cute chicks would pose any danger to me, so I went outside to help them. It was not long before I realised what they were and all bets were off, they all ran back into 3 different directions in the dark - only to then do what I can only describe as a 'floor gymnastics routine' and they began running and front flipping and cart-wheeling towards me (while that mysterious techno beat grew stronger), and as each one reached me I would punch them in the face and they would only disappear from in front me - only to reappear immediately right behind me - and strike me hard. I was growing ever more weary, and they were only getting stronger - like they were feeding off the techno beat rhythm somehow. I knew I was losing - so I cut and ran - but not before one grabbed me by my right foot and slashed my right calf muscle. When I got into the house I shouted to wake up my son, and I felt a burning sensation - so I looked and we both saw that I had 3 bleeding scratches on my right leg calf muscle.

When I was a boy - and into my teens, the sight of evil entities used to scare me, 3-dimensional shadows would strangle me in my sleep often, but as I matured they no longer had that advantage over me psychologically - therefore they could not feed on my fear, so they stopped appearing, until I started to help others with my spiritual gifts, and from then till I learned Usui Reiki and graduated as a practitioner - and began to do actual exorcisms - they REALLY got vengeful towards me, that's when the appearances offering rewards for stopping and serving them instead began.

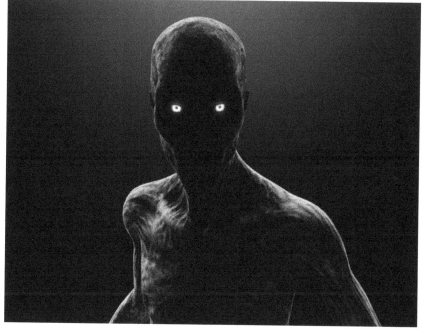

These 3-dimensional shadow demons have appeared to me since my childhood, in our current house, in my uncle house in Puerto Rico, in Guyana, almost everywhere I travelled often, they would be sure to appear at least once to torment me when I was younger, as I did not know or realise at the time - that all lower vibrational entities literally feed on the fear energy you generate when you let such apparitions terrify you.

Nowadays, If/when I see them, I get up and rush towards them as if I want to fight them - and they quickly disappear. Or, if I am too lazy and I'm laying down in bed when one appears, or I hear a growling near my bed coming from some invisible entity, I just say: "Y'all fools are back again to waste your time? "..but other older exorcists think that is being cocky, so they prefer to not respond and merely remain silent, or begin to pray aloud.

Perhaps I am a bit cocky, as they had their fun tormenting me for the first 2 decades of my life, but also..when I first began to learn Reiki, my Master pulled me aside and said she wanted to speak to me privately, she said I have 5 Guardian Angels - and she has never met anyone with so many, she herself has 3, and most humans have 2, a few have just one. "You must have come to do some important spiritual work - to have so many" - she said. So I began to wonder if that was the explanation for my uncanny luck when faced with danger - all my life.

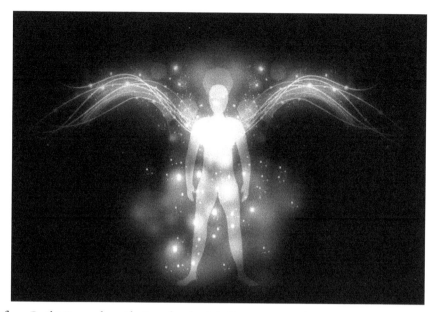

Before Reiki I was heavily involved with financing and participating in my own vigilante justice actions, to help indigenous people who could not get justice any other way - because the Police, Military or Politicians (sometimes all 3) in their own countries - were corrupt and were the ones committing or behind the human rights abuses being inflicted upon them. I wrote a book about those 25 years recently, it's called 'The Amazon is Burning'. Anyway, all the key people who helped me in those actions were men with actual military or police training and combat experience, I am just a person with paramilitary knowledge (partially gained from real veterans close to me), yet I was never harmed on any of these actions, not even a scratch, but all my colleagues are now dead.

———◉———

I once fell off the canopy top of an old ex-British Army Bedford truck in the Jungle - right into the path of the oncoming back wheels, I had fallen flat on my back in a horizontal position, and I remember turning my head to see the back wheels coming straight for my head, I expected to die in the next second as the wind was knocked out of me...but some invisible force picked me up and put me in a standing position at the side of the track - as the wheels passed harmlessly by...I looked around because I felt something hold me and lift me up rapidly, but there was no one else around except the truck driver and the other fellow up on the canopy who was hollering for the driver to stop because I had fallen off.

———— ◉ ————

I have been walking alone, and with my children, and had cars, trucks, motorbikes etc, - lose control and crash right behind or right in front of us, and when I ask the driver what happened - the answer is always similar: "I don't know, it's like some invisible force took control and I could not do anything to stop crashing".

———— ◉ ————

In minor incidents, car tires explode, or something in your home gets thrown down and broken by an invisible force, this is not solely because of demonic infestation, but also when a powerful servant of the darkness such as a Voodoo or Santeria High Priest (as I have dealt with several of them, they claim their beliefs are not evil - yet they permit spiritual vengeance and retribution for perceived wrongs done to them - and this is something NO purely holy spiritual believer EVER sanctions) - directs absolute hateful energy towards you - that evil energy has to work out its fury on something if it cannot touch you (as in my case) - it works out its fury on something nearby instead.

———— ◉ ————

After I broke a spell that a Santeria priest in Cuba helped to put on a young French female tourist who did not really have a strong faith in God, and who he had sending all her money to the man in Cuba, he even bought a car out of it, and he was planning to get her pregnant next, but when I broke the spell she told me she had no idea why she was handing over all her income to this man, and it all started with her taking a drink from him (hiding things in food or drink to control your mind spiritually is a common technique by necromancers). If Santeria was a purely good religion - why does it teach evil things such as this - controlling others to benefit yourself, and casting spells of retaliation against others? Voodoo is the same, basically ANY religion that tells you it is OK to retaliate spiritually or use your esoteric knowledge to control others is EVIL, not good.

So the priest tried to retaliate and harm me (because when you break an evil spell - the sender senses it immediately and they find out who broke it from the evil spirits they serve, as we are constantly under observation by both higher and lower entities.

One bit of potentially useful advice that works for me, is whenever anyone gives you food to eat or a beverage to drink, say these words (because words have more power than thoughts from a spiritual point of view...as thought becomes word - which then manifests into reality) over the food or drink before you consume any of it: "May the intent of the sender return to them", So in this way, if the person giving you the food or drink did so with a heart of love and blessings for you - love and blessings shall return to them, but if they did so with ill intentions - their ill intentions will return to them - for as Jesus said 'everyone must reap just as they have sown in this life'. Do good and you shall receive good, but if you do bad - bad shall you receive. This is the neutral beauty of Universal karmic justice, whatever YOU do in your loaned life - you will have to accept responsibility for, both good and ill.

Nothing we do in our physical body vehicle is truly done in secret - and that's why you get deceived by evil entities via Ouija boards, they saw and heard everything your deceased loved one said and did in life - so they can pretend to be them very convincingly, and because you desperately WANT to believe that it is really the soul or spirit of your physically deceased (but still immortal conscious energy living) loved one - you fall for their convincing trap...and you unwittingly open a portal in your home for lower vibrational entities to enter into your lives from inside your own home.

Just because no other human saw what we did - remember the spirit world sees everything, so I have had truly bizarre cases of pets being killed in mysterious ways, a dog using its chain to strangle another dog, a rabbit alone in a locked cage with no signs of wire damage or entry, having its head ripped off inside the locked cage, fires erupting on furniture in the garage out of nowhere - with no fuel or other accelerant or source of combustion anywhere nearby.

———— ❧ ————

People with no belief in God and no knowledge of esoteric realities are easy victims.

———— ❧ ————

An invisible force knocking you down and things that cannot be casually explained away will occur, but if you do not have the stomach for the backlash, do not get yourself involved in this kind of spiritual warfare, in exorcisms prayers are like flu shots, they don't provide immunity - only reduced risk, and all the best exorcists have been physically harmed when working.

However, Reiki AND my traditional Tribal Shamanic teachings - teach me that It is NEVER right or good to wish or send any negative spiritual energy to anyone, I break Voodoo and Santeria priests harmful spells, but I do not desire or wish any harm upon those people who do spiritual wickedness, I can only try to send love and light into their hearts and minds in the attempt to turn them away from their service to the darkness.

———◉———

On a side note, when I say I am a lightworker like my father, I do not mean my father was also an Usui Reiki practitioner or possessor of Shamanic knowledge like me, dads paternal heritage leads back to western Europe, mums maternal heritage leads back to Amazonia, I just happen to be their only child that always self identified with my Amazonian Indian heritage, while my siblings went in our fathers ancestral direction.

I call my dad (and mum also) 'Light workers' because they led exemplary lives of good, always kind, peaceful, loving, caring, generous, decent, morally upstanding parents.

———◉———

My parents were married for 60 faithful years, no affairs or 'outside children', my dad was my mothers first and only boyfriend, husband and lover, and I never once in my 47 years of life living with my parents (as its traditional in indigenous societies for one child to take care of their parents when they get old and less capable) - did my father and mother ever hit each other, or even utter cuss words at each other, nor did they ever get drunk, mum never liked the taste of alcohol, and one beer a day was enough for dad.

———◉———

Dad also became an orphan at age 9 when he lost both his parents, but he never 'acted up' and needed therapy or counselling like kids today who experience early childhood trauma, dad and his older brother realised and accepted that they now had the responsibility to take care of their 4 younger siblings - and from the time they could legally find jobs - that's exactly what they did, how many children do you know who were so selfless and mentally mature at such a young age?

———◉———

Another anomaly was that my dad and his siblings never once got into a fight with each other, and (unlike me and my siblings who all got into fights) dad never got into a single fight with anyone nor had any enemy he was aware of - his entire 87 years of life!

———◉———

He never hit us either . All of these reasons mark this role model of a true human being as a 'lightworker' as far as I am concerned. If everyone took responsibility for their own actions - and stopped blaming everyone else for their messed up life, there would be no absentee fathers, wife beaters, child molesters, and broken families all over this world, because everyone would realise that the greatest of all foundations in the life of any human being - is to be raised surrounded by LOVE in their own home first and foremost.

———◉———

Getting back to my supernatural tribulations, the next day my wife came into the room where I was sleeping, and she saw dozens of big black crows, the kind native to North America and Europe - NOT the Caribbean, surrounding my bed and looking at me, cackling among themselves as if waiting for something, but suddenly they disappeared and I opened my eyes, then my wife told me what she had just seen, "they are waiting to feast on my dead flesh, as they ever did to the corpses of the dead on battlefields of old"...I told her intuitively.

However, THIS was the spiritual catalyst that gave me the drive to fight back and defeat this illness, as I no longer saw it as a mere physical battle, but there was obviously a spiritual dimension to this war to survive as well. As the forces of darkness were hoping for my imminent death in my virus weakened status.

I don't say that lightly, but ever since I became a Usui Reiki level 3 Practitioner, and I began to use myself as a conduit to run natural energy into others with various physical or supernatural issues, and the victims of these things healed, every so often dark entities would appear to me and tell me to "stop doing this work, if you serve the darkness you will receive fame, fortune, women - anything you want - in abundance for the rest of your life", but I always answer them the same way by saying "I am a servant of the light like my father before me, and I will never serve the darkness - no matter what you do to my body - because you cannot touch my soul"....then they always threaten me by saying "we will persecute you for the rest of your life and make sure you suffer until your last breath".

———— ◉ ————

It felt to me on my worst night in the second week of my combined viral and spiritual tribulation, that my last breath was not that far away if I gave up hope and faith.

———— ◉ ————

Many fall for the temporary gains such as are always offered, we see MANY celebrities who have done so, we all know them, and the forces of darkness do keep their word - in the sense that 'for the rest of your life' you WILL enjoy fame, fortune, wanton lust and unbridled hedonism (things the spiritually dead majority of humanity consider to be 'heaven on Earth'), etc..but those who sell their souls always assume that they will enjoy a long life...yet they never do, 'the rest of your life' could be days, months or just a few years after you have sealed your fate.

They never guarantee you a long life, because they cannot, only God has the power to decide the number of our days on Earth, but once you seal your fate with the dark forces, they DO have the power and authority to shorten the number of your days, and it was you who granted them this right over you!

———— ◉ ————

I feel only pity for such short-sighted people, they are not yet old souls (like my father) who are wise enough to know that a human lifetime is but a split-second of cosmic time. Why trade eternity for a few decades? Or as Jesus said "what profit is there to gain the whole world - and lose your own soul?"

You may ask what is the difference between young souls and old souls?

Well in a nutshell, look around this world, and everyone you see who is creating lower vibrational (aka negative) problems for the Earth and all its inhabitants - is a young (and ignorant) soul, and everyone you see who is creating higher vibrational (aka positive) solutions for the Earth and all its inhabitants - is an old (and wiser) soul.

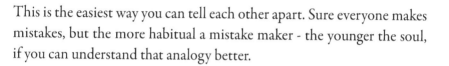

This is the easiest way you can tell each other apart. Sure everyone makes mistakes, but the more habitual a mistake maker - the younger the soul, if you can understand that analogy better.

So don't hate anyone, merely recognise where their spiritual evolution is at - in their current incarnation. In time they will become wise old souls as well, we all will.

CHAPTER 5

I remembered that over one year before, in mid-2020, I had told my older brother Craig of a premonition dream I had, in which I contracted this virus and it took me near to death - but then I conquered it and recovered, so rearmed with the knowledge that I had ALREADY foreseen my victorious outcome, I was re-energized mentally and spiritually, and I also began to get help and assistance from a distance from my Usui Reiki Master back in Barbados, who was contacted by my wife unbeknown to myself.

———— ◉ ————

I did not tell ANYONE in my family up to that point, as I do not like to bother people with my personal problems, especially people that already are running their own gamut of stress factors in their own lives, like my big-hearted mum, and my big sister Lisa, or my very busy older brothers who are running successful businesses in very difficult times.

———— ◉ ————

The first family members I told were my 3 children who were not with me, my eldest Son Hatuey and second son Tecumseh (both in Barbados), and my elder daughter Sabantho in Sweden (where she recently got married), all of whom have varying degrees of spiritual connection to me, and they see things in dreams concerning me (and vice-versa) before they are informed by me or anyone else in our tangible reality.

———— ◉ ————

For example, my firstborn son Hatuey (back in Barbados) was the first to contact me BEFORE I said a word to him about any of the supernatural incidents, or even that I had the crown virus, and he told me he had 2 dreams in the same second week of August when my symptoms were most severe, and he saw that dark entities were eagerly anticipating my death. In fact, in his dream state - he defeated a Demon that was sent against me - and that coincided with my recovery beginning the next dawn.

———————⬤———————

Sabantho in Sweden was the second to tell me she was seeing spiritual danger for me from dark entities who were now targeting me...and remember - this is all BEFORE I told them anything.

Even my Reiki master detected the same - totally independent of my kids, and my kids detected it totally independent of each other, and both myself and my wife saw supernatural things totally independent of each other as well, what are the odds of 5 different people in 3 different countries - all privately seeing the same thing without communicating with each other - only with me?

———◉———

Anyway, this is when I also began to increase my consumption of natural remedies, besides the water, herbal tea, and the fruit only diet - I began to take a tablespoon of honey every day, eat a diced pod of garlic every day, and drink a tablespoon of lemon juice with a half teaspoon of salt every day, drink peppermint tea and ginger tea every day, and stand outside in the morning to get 15 minutes of direct sunlight on my skin - to get the very important vitamin D3 as well, every morning around 9am.

———◉———

I like to hike, so even early in this second week of severe discomfort, I still pushed myself to do a night hike for 5 hours up the nearby St Peters Hill in Sint Maarten with my daughter and wife, even though I could not walk briskly as I normally do, only take slower steps, and even so I was breathing rapidly and loudly through my mouth - as my nose was not giving me enough air.

———◉———

I also had to stop every 30 minutes and lean up against a tree, or sit on a large stone, just to catch my breath for 15 minutes, so this same 2 hr 30 minute hike I did with my daughter Laliwa 8 times before - now took twice as long. But I feel good that even on the verge of suffocating - I was still strong enough to do a hike up and down a mountain that is over 1,000 feet above sea level (according to the Nature Foundation of Sint Maarten) Nature Foundation Hillside data for Sint Maarten[1]

---

1. https://naturefoundationsxm.org/2016/04/13/hillsides/

CHAPTER 6

I refused to go to any Doctor, or Nurse, or Clinic or Hospital, because I was worried that all three of us would be taken and placed in some facility somewhere, maybe even separated, and the fact that we were not going out of the house anyway - so not putting anyone in the public at risk of whatever the hell it was that I had, I decided to stay under the radar in our rented house, and just continue to fight this battle alone among ourselves, with no modern medicines whatsoever either, as I was never a pill-popper or a trusting devotee of the Pharmaceutical Industry.

———◉———

I trust in nature as it is still as pure as God made it, why depend on synthetic chemical replicas of natural plant extracts - if you can still get the God-made natural plant directly? Makes no sense to me!

———◉———

I have a sister-in-law who died of liver and kidney failure - from years of taking a cocktail of 6 different man-made chemical pills daily, one tablet was for this, but it caused side effects in that, and the tablet for that, caused side effects in this, and so it went...I told her in March 2018 'If you continue taking these chemical pills - you will be dead within two years, she died in February 2020, still trusting in man-made medicine - and doubting natural God-made remedies.

———◉———

When I have a headache - I never take a single pill, I merely chew nuts, or massage under the soles of my feet (just as one natural remedy example), and the headache ends, if I have a chest cough, I drink a tablespoon of lemon juice with a half teaspoon of salt, it clears the mucous away, or I drink peppermint tea - it also clears mucus away, allowing you to breathe better. Pure natural honey is a great natural antibiotic not to be underestimated, likewise garlic.

All this time I was fighting this alone with only my wife and daughter physically with me to help me, I did not know at the time for sure it was the 'crown' virus, so on Friday 27th August, we all went to the top Laboratory & virus test facility in Sint Maarten, to have our tests done. We were all supposed to fly back home on Sunday 29th August, but upon collecting the results I was told that the virus was detected in me so I could not travel for another week IF my next test was negative, though my wife and daughter who were sharing a close personal space with me - were both negative.

My daughter more than once had taken a sip from a cup I was drinking from, and my wife was sleeping next to me every night in the same bed - yet the supposedly highly contagious virus did not touch them, the only thing I did towards this end to protect them - was to put an energetic spiritual cocoon around them and ask the Universe to protect them from being infected.

This may sound silly on the surface, but one of the Reiki masters I know put just such an energetic shield around his house before a hurricane, and everyone else's home surrounding him was either damaged or destroyed, but his remained completely untouched in even the most minor way, so perhaps it is not as silly as you seem.

I also have seen - and achieved myself, running natural energy into skeptical people with physical pain - muscular or joint issues (including arthritis), and after running natural energy into them - in minutes their pain is gone. In fact, I do this for my own 82-year-old mother often.

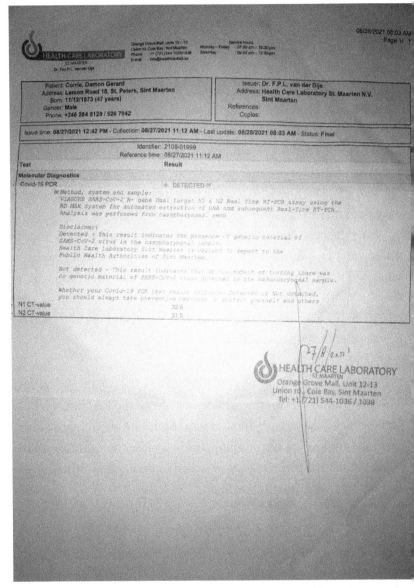

My positive test result proof in Sint Maarten that I collected on 28th
August 2021

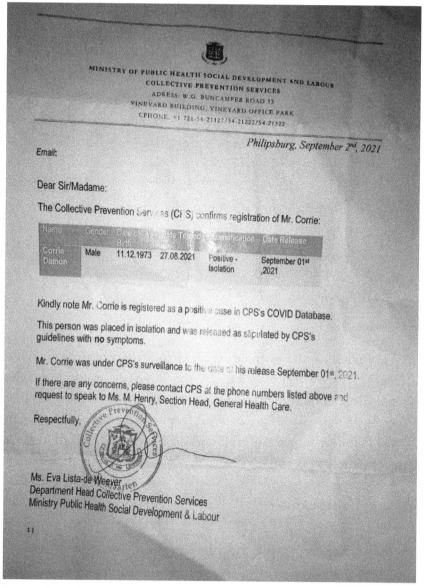

MINISTRY OF PUBLIC HEALTH SOCIAL DEVELOPMENT AND LABOUR
COLLECTIVE PREVENTION SERVICES
ADRESS: W.G. BUNCAMPER ROAD 33
VINEYARD BUILDING, VINEYARD OFFICE PARK
CPHONE: +1 721-54-21127/54-21222/54-21322

Philipsburg, September 2nd, 2021

Email:

Dear Sir/Madame:

The Collective Prevention Services (CPS) confirms registration of Mr. Corrie:

Name	Gender	Date of Birth	Date Tested	Classification	Date Release
Corrie Damon	Male	11.12.1973	27.08.2021	Positive - Isolation	September 01st ,2021

Kindly note Mr. Corrie is registered as a positive case in CPS's COVID Database.

This person was placed in isolation and was released as stipulated by CPS's guidelines with **no symptoms**.

Mr. Corrie was under CPS's surveillance to the date of his release September 01st, 2021.

If there are any concerns, please contact CPS at the phone numbers listed above and request to speak to Ms. M. Henry, Section Head, General Health Care.

Respectfully,

Ms. Eva Lista-de Weever
Department Head Collective Prevention Services
Ministry Public Health Social Development & Labour

Letter from Sint Maarten authorities preventing me from travelling out of their country

My biggest personal proof and source of joy hitherto, was running natural energy into my own father-in-law, to clear his lungs of excess fluid, which every private and public hospital in Guyana had tried to cure with the latest man-made medicines - but could not, and they eventually all told him that his case was 'incurable at his advanced age'.

———◉———

So since medical science had given up on him, I decided to try using natural energy on him - as he literally had nothing else to lose.

———◉———

I spent an hour running natural energy into my father-in-law's lungs - all the while visualizing the fluid in his lungs evaporating, and his lungs becoming as healthy as they were when he was half his age - in his thirties, I focussed with all my being on saving him, till tears of love ran down my cheeks, as he was my second father.

———◉———

He was healed, and when he went back to all those medical experts - they were perplexed that his chest Xrays now showed healthy lungs clear of fluid, some mumbled that it must be a miracle, but it was not, just natural energy doing what it was always meant to do, and my father-in-law had the following three years of normal breathing until just before he died - when it returned, and because of the Pandemic - I was not able to travel to work on him again in time.

———◉———

Another useful everyday tip I can share with you, is that water is the holiest liquid you can ever consume, but if it is polluted - naturally from a biological health perspective, it will not be so good for you to consume.

———◉———

There are still things you can do though, firstly - never drink water straight from the tap, even if it is not polluted, that water that comes out is in a state of near cellular obliteration - after having been forcefully slammed into multiple bends in the pipes that took it from the pumping station - to your kitchen sink.

———◉———

No, let that water collect in a jar, or mug, or some other bulk liquid receptacle for several hours (preferable overnight) BEFORE you consume it, this allows the water molecules to reform, and you can then basically add to the natural energy value status of that water by speaking to it with as many spiritually positive words as come to mind, I like to say ' Love, Peace, Joy, Bliss, Contentment, Gratitude, Honor, Kindness, Generosity, etc' to my water before I consume it, you would be surprised to know that under a powerful microscope - those water molecules transform into beautiful crystalline shapes like snowflakes and basically becomes 'holy'. Your priest does the same thing.

CHAPTER 7

You see, 'Reiki' is merely the Japanese word for 'Natural Energy', it is the life force in all things, that unites us in a universal cosmic energy field of creation, every holy man, shaman, traditional healer, etc, even Jesus - used this to heal others, there are no magic words that affect the healing, only love and concern from the conduit for the recipient, if you have no love in you for humanity and other life forms, you cannot be a successful conduit for natural energy, there are certain miracles that Jesus (for example) performed that I cannot explain, such as walking on water, etc, but the healing of the sick - and even raising the dead - I can explain and I do understand as natural energy.

———— ◦ ————

Jesus was a million times better and more divine and perfect at conduiting this for the healing of others, that is why he could even resurrect a recently dead man (Lazarus) whom he personally knew and loved.

———— ◦ ————

I only realized this when my own Reiki master brought a recently killed monkey back to life, it was a fresh road kill, struck by a car, was bleeding from its mouth, nose and ears, no vital signs, no breath, nothing, but after 30 minutes of my Master holding it and lovingly running natural energy into it (as she had witnessed the vehicle kill it) - it came back to life and ran away into the trees.

———— ◦ ————

In my own life, I was brought a dead lizard by my kids who had accidentally killed it, I put it underwater for 3 minutes to see if it was still breathing, nothing, I took it out and put a flame to it, no reaction, so I put it in my hands and began to focus natural energy on it, my hands eventually grew very warm, and near to 10 minutes into this my hands began to glow a bright yellow, then I felt movement in my hands,

I opened them and the lizard was alive, breathing and looking around as if nothing ever happened.

So I took it outside and released it on a tree, what joy to see it scurry away!

———◉———

So these are the incidents that allowed me to understand the reason why someone as divine as Jesus would resurrect a human being, for lesser mortals such as we - can bring dead freshly killed small animals back to life.

———◉———

It is just a matter of natural energy returning to their cells - before too much damage and decay has occurred.

However, I believe only the holy creative macro-consciousness force of love and light itself that we call God - could reanimate long-dead physical bodies such as several religions describe in their resurrection teachings.

———◉———

For me personally, I think it would make more sense to just use the already immortal conscious energy selves/souls we all have, why the need to re-animate our more restrictive human body vehicles anyhow?

———◉———

Been there-done that, on numerous occasions, I might add...no need to return us into the 'school for the soul' (which is what our body vehicles are - mere avatars for our true energetic selves to use for a brief blip in cosmic time) when we have already graduated from it - is there?

———◉———

Take caution though, because not every Reiki Master or Practitioner is 'kosher' as the Jews say, I know of one Reiki Master who started off the right way in humility, but his growing success and fame made his ego emerge quite forcefully and take over his being, he began to say HE healed this person or that person when in reality every true Reiki student knows that we do nothing ourselves - except conduit the universal natural life force energy through us and back into another body, where it is no longer flowing as normally and healthily as it should be, only the love of God truly heals anyone.

———— ◉ ————

So when you notice a 'healer' taking personal credit for the healings that occur - beware!

For this 'healer' has been consumed by ego, and no longer is a genuine lightworker, but merely a corrupted one.

Patients may still obtain relief, but the practitioner is sooner or later going to fall into shadow - with his/her ego leading the way to their ultimate downfall, and perhaps yours too - if you blindly follow them.

———— ◉ ————

Just because a person appears to perform what you consider to be 'miraculous healings, does not always mean this is 'proof' that they are a lightworker, any Jews, Christians, or Muslim brothers or sisters reading this will recall that the Magicians of Pharoah were ALSO able to turn their wooden staffs into snakes - just like Moses.

So remember that example when you see charlatans like the popular multi-millionaire televangelists who dominate the 'religious' channels on TV and their carefully micro-managed stage shows - in their run-for-profit businesses they call 'houses of God'.

If they were truly able to perform miracles - how come they only do it on their own stages?

Why not wander the streets (or enter any hospital anywhere) doing random miracles in public as Jesus did?

Because they cannot - because they are all opportunistic frauds who are masters of deception and illusion only.

I know that someone who ONLY does Reiki for a living, will obviously - and understandably - have to charge you a fee for their work on you.

However, even though I am a self-employed person, with a roller-coaster income, one month I may do very well, the next month I may literally earn not a single cent..I still do NOT charge anyone I do natural energy work on anything.

Then again, I usually only do Reiki on poor people who I know cannot afford to pay, and in the back of my mind, I always remember that my father and mother ALWAYS told me, any spiritual ability to help others is a gift from God so you should not ask for monetary compensation or payment.

It is our traditional ancestral spirituality way, to NOT give money in exchange for spiritual help, but to still show appreciation in other ways - such as offering Tobacco, sage, fruit, food, sacred stones or crystals, woodcarvings, basketry, a hammock, something - as to expect to receive help for free is not an honorable way to live, always offer an exchange - it shows humility and respect.

———◉———

The MAIN spiritual lesson I would wish everyone to take from having read this humble literary effort of mine, is to harbour less ego, less judgmentalism, less fear, and less hatred in your hearts and minds, and instead replace it with, humility, love and tolerance for your fellow human beings - your spiritual brothers and sisters, no matter how difficult it is to see them in this lens of spiritual truth; for in the end - LOVE shall conquer all.

———◉———

In the end, we all tested negative for the virus on the test we took 7 days later - after it was detected in me in my recovery week, and we flew back home to Barbados island, where we were all put in a government decreed mandatory 7 days quarantine - despite arriving with negative virus tests, if it were Sint Maarten - that would have been enough to allow a visitor to walk out of the airport and begin enjoying their precious and limited holiday time - right away.

———◉———

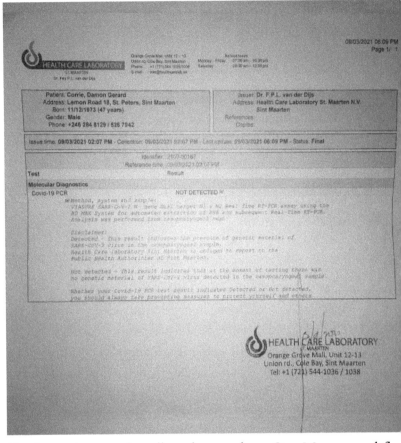

My Final negative test that allowed me to leave Sint Maarten and fly home to Barbados

I thank you for purchasing my humble book, I hope it gave you some food for thought, and if not a laugh, at least a smile at some points, and an increased sense of hope that we can and WILL beat this pandemic in more ways than one, and eventually we - as a species, will become more united and less divided than we are exhibiting presently, to my disappointment.

———◉———

If some aspect of this book has peaked your anthropological, spiritual, or literary interest, please consider visiting the following:

On Instagram @eagleclanarawaks
My website at -Eagle Clan Arawaks[1]
My blog site at -Eagle Clan Arawaks blog[2]

1.   https://eagleclanarawaks.com/

2.   https://wordpress.com/posts/eagleclanarawaks.com

Don't miss out!

Visit the website below and you can sign up to receive emails whenever Damon Corrie publishes a new book. There's no charge and no obligation.

https://books2read.com/r/B-A-ADZI-ZEASB

BOOKS 2 READ

Connecting independent readers to independent writers.

Did you love *Confessions of a Reiki Exorcist*? Then you should read *Dream State Experiences*[3] by Damon Corrie!

If you usually depend on 'dream interpretation' websites, this book will open your eyes to an entirely new reality aspect to dreams and dreaming - hitherto not covered by anyone to the breadth and scope of Damon's personal experiences.

While he does recognize that 'dream symbolism' can apply to most human beings 'dreams', they do not explain the category that Damon routinely experiences,

Damon Gerard Corrie's 'dreams' are frequent (often 3 per night every night of the year), vividly detailed, have accurately predicted future events with their precognition qualities - including the death of his first daughter as a baby long before she was even physically conceived yet, so

3. https://books2read.com/u/bzegNq

4. https://books2read.com/u/bzegNq

forget what you THINK you may know about the phenomena referred to as 'dreaming' - which Damon prefers to describe as 'Dream state experiences'. His are on an entirely new level.

After you have read this selection of less than one years worth of his over 40 years of remembered experiences, you may have to rethink everything that you thought you knew before - about this fascinating subject matter. From Film Industry writers and paranormal authors to scientific researchers and the average spiritually inclined/curious person, all have found Damon's experiences to be a mind-expanding and thought-provoking read.

Some go so far as to say that they have learned more about the afterlife in just one hour of reading about Damon's dream state experiences - than they have learned from their own religions and religious texts in their entire lifetimes.

Separated into 49 individual accounts (as the numbers 4 & 9 are sacred numbers in traditional Lokono-Arawak spirituality & cosmovision), this volume represents less than 5% of the 'dream state experiences Damon has annually.

Read more at https://www.facebook.com/shamanchief/.

Also by Damon Corrie

Life Lessons Series
Understanding Spirituality, Anomalous Phenomena as life lessons
Understanding Spirituality, Dreams, Insights, Exorcisms, Visitations
and Shamanic Healing
Dream State Experiences

Standalone
The Amazon is Burning - The Flames of 21st Century Resistance
Inspired by Indigenous Women
Amazonia's Mythical and Legendary Creatures in the Eagle Clan
Lokono-Arawak Oral Tradition of Guyana
Lokono-Arawaks
The Last Arawak girl born in Barbados - A 17th Century Tale
Confessions of a Reiki Exorcist
A Phonetic English to Arawak Dictionary

Watch for more at https://www.facebook.com/shamanchief/.

About the Author

Damon, like his 3 older siblings, was born on the Caribbean island of Barbados. His mother Audrey named Damon after the American author Damon Runyon, and from a very young age Damon exhibited a passion and love for writing; however, like most aspiring authors Damon found it impossible to share his manuscripts with a broader audience (until he discovered draft2digital), so for over 3 decades his many works in many genres gathered dust on his bookshelf of unfulfilled dreams.

Damon is a 4th generation descendant of the last traditional Hereditary Shaman Chief Amorothe Haubariria (Flying Harpy Eagle) of the Bariria Korobahado Lokono (Eagle Clan Arawaks) of Guyana, South America, Moreover, the grave of Damon's great grandmother is the only known burial site of a member of Lokono-Arawak nobility in the entire Caribbean - and with a tombstone written in both the English and Lokono-Arawak language, it has become a tourist attraction in the Westbury Cemetery in the capital city of Bridgetown Barbados.

Damon has the gift of premonition dreams and being able to see and communicate with deceased loved ones, and since he married back into the tribe at the age of 19 in 1992, Damon has become the most radical indigenous activists the Caribbean has produced in living memory, and his real-life escapades and supernatural experiences feature in his writings.

Damon was a member of the Caribbean Caucus on the Indigenous Peoples working group of the Organization of American States (OAS) from 2000 to 2016, and helped create the Declaration of The Americas on the Rights of Indigenous Peoples, and he has been a registered participant of the United Nations Permanent Forum on Indigenous Issues (UNPFII) since 2007 (where he also co-mentors international students and writes for the Tribal Link Foundation), as well as being an autodidact journalist with news articles published in 4 continents, and a writer for the Last Real Indians indigenous media website.

Damon (46) and his wife Shirling (44) have 4 living children, sons Hatuey Francis (26) and Tecumseh Shawandase (23), and daughters Sabantho Aderi (20) and Laliwa Hadali, and all live in Barbados. Damon can be followed in Instagram @eagleclanarawaks

Read more at https://www.facebook.com/shamanchief/.

About the Publisher

Lightning Source UK Ltd.
Milton Keynes UK
UKHW050018151221
395665UK00015B/391